MEETING JESUS ON LIFE'S JOURNEY
– A poetry collection

In memory of Mum and Dad, Jean and Hugh Murphy.

Thanks for keeping the report cards, Dad. They were an inspiration.

Alison Murphy

Published by New Generation Publishing in 2018
Copyright © Alison Murphy 2018

First Edition

The author asserts the moral right under the Copyright, Designs and Patents Act 1988 to be identified as the author of this work.

All Rights reserved. No part of this publication may be reproduced, stored in a retrieval system or transmitted, in any form or by any means without the prior consent of the author, nor be otherwise circulated in any form of binding or cover other than that which it is published and without a similar condition being imposed on the subsequent purchaser.

All Bible references used are from the New International Version®, NIV® Copyright ©1973, 1978, 1984, 2011 by Biblica. All rights reserved worldwide.

www.newgeneration-publishing.com

Contents

PART ONE – PEOPLE WHO MET JESUS 1

    The Innkeeper's first Christmas 3

    Joseph learns the truth behind Isaiah 55:9 5

    Mary ponders 7

    The Angel's Commission 9

    A shepherd remembers. 11

    A Wise Man's reflections 13

    Nativity and After... Fulfilment of Promise. 15

    Anna rejoices... 17

    Zebedee is deserted 19

    Just five loaves and a couple of fish 21

    The Bridegroom comes 23

    Belovèd Zacchaeus 25

    Living Water 27

    Bartimaeus gets his heart's desire 29

    Jairus' hope is tested 31

    Lazarus, Come Forth 33

    A song on Palm Sunday 35

    Malchus recalls 38

    Barabbas is pardoned... 41

    Pilate's dilemma 44

    Simon's story 47

    An Arimathean Miracle – Joseph finds his courage. 50

    The Centurion's story 53

    What Cleopas learned on the road to Emmaus 55

    Peter finds forgiveness 57

PART TWO – ENJOY THE JOURNEY 61

   Valentine's Day 63

   Once.. 65

   When the Sparrow Falls... 67

   In every Wilderness. 69

   The Storm - Walking on Water 71

   A little deadly weapon 73

   What kind of light are you? 75

   Who are you, Lord? 77

PART ONE – PEOPLE WHO MET JESUS

The Innkeeper's first Christmas

"So many people and all wanting fed,
they've come for the census and I've not a bed.
There's so much to do and I'm feeling quite stressed,
with no time to stop for a wee bit of rest.

A couple from Nazareth here at my door,
I'm sorry we're full, there's no room for one more.
But the woman's with child and her time has now come,
I can't let them go and so what's to be done?

The stable is free; I can let them stay there,
though it's not ideal, of that I'm aware.
But at least it will make sure they're out of the cold,
for the poor lass is beat and she's not very old.

Her child is a son and he's such a fine boy,
I'm sure he'll do well, bring his parents real joy.
Now some shepherds appear, they've seen angels they say –
Oh, what a miracle, oh what a day!

And here are some wise men, they've travelled far,
to worship this child, they have followed a star.
They've brought him fine gifts for they say he's a king,
He was born in my stable who'd have thought such a thing!

I'm no longer weary, and there's so much to ponder,
When young Jesus grows up, what will happen I wonder..."

...2000 years later, are you also so busy?
Have you still lots to do; are you all in a tizzy?
Well, stop for a second and I'll finish the story –
what the innkeeper saw, it was all for God's glory.

You see, we know now what he didn't know then,
that the Child had been born to be Saviour to men.
That He'd grow in wisdom, do marvellous things.
And the wise men were right – for He would be a king.

Though with none of the trappings that go with that role,
He touched lives that were broken and He made them whole.
He made sick people well and raised lives from the dead,
and then on a cross died for our sins instead.

The innkeeper looked forward in wonder and hope,
now that hope is ours, Christ will help us to cope.
In the year that's ahead, He will help us through,
For you see He loves us, yes that's right – me and you!

His message of hope is so needed today,
Be like the innkeeper don't turn Him away.

Luke Chapter 2: 6-7. While they were there, the time came for the baby to be born, and she gave birth to her firstborn, a son. She wrapped him in cloths and placed him in a manger, because there was no guest room available for them.

Joseph learns the truth behind Isaiah 55:9

*"As the heavens are higher
than the earth, so are my ways higher than your ways and my thoughts
than your thoughts."*

"A quiet celebration was just not what I had planned;
I wanted something special when I asked for Mary's hand.
Something unexpected happened that sent all my plans askew,
and my mind was in a quandary, I did not know what to do.

But then I had a visitor – an angel of all folk,
I fell on my knees and trembled as I heard the words he spoke.
Mary hadn't been unfaithful and her Child would be God's Son,
sent to the world as Saviour, to reach each and everyone.

And so we married; quietly, but then came another blow,
there had to be a census - to Bethlehem we'd go.
Just as the birth grew nearer, all my plans awry again,
for there was no room to take us - what was to happen then?

We were finally offered shelter, in a stable for a night.
This wasn't what I wanted for the birth; it wasn't right!
But our little One, Immanuel, arrived and we were blessed,
even though the circumstances put us really to the test.

That night we had more visitors, shepherds sent from off the plain,
by a company of angels and we all rejoiced again.
Though my plans all came to nothing for God's plans more great than mine,
and our new born baby, Jesus, truly was divine.

He would grow to save His people, turning many back to God,
but the way this was accomplished would to others just seem odd.
I really didn't understand all it seemed that God had planned,
though I learned that I could trust Him, with this Child all was in hand."

Whatever we are planning, our plans too may go askew,
but like Joseph we can trust God for He knows just what to do.
And that baby in the stable – just how did the story end? -
Jesus grew to be our Saviour and He wants to be our friend.

Mary ponders

"This Child of mine, helpless and small,
the Angel said is Lord of all.
My baby boy, God's Son, he said.
Such thoughts awhirl within my head.

I do not fully understand,
dear Joseph feels the same.
But in Jehovah God we trust,
Jesus then is our Son's name.

Some shepherds came and told us
Angels had appeared to them,
Proclaiming peace and joy, henceforth,
Goodwill from God to men.

Later some highly learned men,
who'd travelled far and wide,
told us they had found us
with just a star to guide.

They brought us gifts so precious,
and they knelt before my Son.
It seems that God had shown them too
He was the Chosen One.

He sleeps so peacefully just now,
I wonder is it really so?
What things await us years ahead,
as I watch my dear Son grow?

I will always be His mother,
I might worry some, or fret.
But the things that I have seen thus far
I never will forget."

It took just more than 30 years
for these things to unfold,
but Mary saw God's promises
were true as she'd been told.

She knew great grief and then great joy,
as she watched God's plan fulfilled.
Her Saviour Son, at greatest cost,
would do His Father's will.

God's plans are never hurried,
and His promises still true.
I hope this little poem
Makes you ponder this anew.

When we celebrate each Christmas,
let it be as it was then.
Let's take time to seek the Saviour,
And make peace with fellow men.

Luke Chapter 2: 18-20: "And all who heard it were amazed at what the shepherds said to them. ***But Mary treasured up all these things and pondered them in her heart.*** The shepherds returned, glorifying and praising God for all they had heard and seen, which was just as the angel had told them."

Sometimes God's promises take a while to come to pass and we have to keep reminding ourselves of them. However, even if they take a decade or more, they are ALWAYS fulfilled!

The Angel's Commission

¹"The time has come," my Master said," to go and tell the world."
My joy could hardly be contained as I knelt with wings unfurled.
"Now go and tell my people that I have sent my Son,
to live and grow amongst them, show my love to everyone."

So off I went to David's town, it was the dead of night,
the shepherds on the hillside then were stunned with fear and fright.
"Fear not," I said, "Good news I bring,
To you this day is born a King."

"Not in grand home, but stable lowly,
the Son of God, a Babe most holy."
Other angels joined me then, we filled the hills with praise,
the shepherds went to Bethlehem, their minds still in a daze.

They found Him, as I said they would,
my Master cannot lie.
And I pondered at a distance on that baby, born to die.
For I, though mighty angel, could not fully understand,
what God the Father had revealed, though

knew all was in hand.'

'Tis true that like the angel,
we might puzzle at God's plan.
But like the shepherds need not fear,
For Jesus with us will stand.

Now when fears come at dead of night,
and we like shepherds cower in fright,
The Christ Himself will light our way,
Turn what is dark to light of day.

And so just like the angels,
Let us take the time to praise,
The Son, now grown remains with us
And will be all our days.

Read the full record in **Luke chapter 2: 10-20.**

A shepherd remembers.

"I'm just a young shepherd, paid to watch sheep,
sometimes in the dark, whilst most folks are asleep.
It's not the best job for our status is low,
and when it's quiet the time goes so slow.

We're not highly thought of but we stick together,
looking after our sheep, whatever the weather.
The sheep – lowly animals, some born to die,
our substitute sacrifice for sin and lies.

One evening I met with some friends round a fire,
we could never have guessed just what would transpire.
An angel from Heaven before us appeared,
so terribly awesome, we were done for I feared.

But 'fear not,' he told us, 'it's good news that I bring,
go to Bethlehem now where you'll find a new King.'
Before our eyes next, heavenly host then sang out,
"All glory to God," they declared with a shout.

But then when they'd gone, what could this all mean?
Was it really all true or just simply a dream?
We headed off to Bethlehem to find the baby King,
and we found him in a stable, in a manger of all things.

For you see the angel told us we would find the Lamb of God,
Who would grow up wise in stature but would in our footsteps trod.
For one day too, He would become our sacrifice for sin,
but once, and for all people - and many lives He'd win.

What wonder was this and revealed first to us,
While Bethlehem slept on without any fuss.
My life turned around on that dark winter night,
For my heart had lit up at that wonderful sight.

And my attitude changed, I'm now different you see,
since I now understand that God loves even me."

And so, not just at Christmas, I wish you great joy,
but would ask you remember that young shepherd boy.
We might be a shepherd; we may be a king,
We may not have much, or perhaps many things.

The shepherd boy's story, though wondrous is true,
God sent His Son, Jesus for me and for you.

The shepherd's story is also found in **Luke Chapter 2: 8-12.**

A Wise Man's reflections

We were thought to be wise – studied stars, many maps;
So, to find a new star, no surprise then perhaps?
And yet this one was different, we all felt the same –
wondered what was its purpose, the reason it came?

Somehow compelled we set off in its wake,
with no thought for the impact our journey would make.
'Twas the sign of a King we decided, for sure,
as each night we followed its dazzling allure.

But where would it lead us, our homage to pay?
We mused as we purchased fine gifts on our way.
Israel so it seemed was to be journey's end,
where we went first to Herod who we thought was a friend.

But we knew when he spoke he did not understand,
that this newly born King would rule more than the land.
A few more days further we found the new Babe,
When the star finally stopped at the place where He laid.

And I knew when I saw Him, with a wisdom not mine
He would grow truly wise – make His mark for all time.
Though I'd achieved much and had seen many things
I am glad that I followed the star to this King."

What became of that King and what mark did He make?
The Bible says - born to die just for our sake.
Though the star shines no longer, signs of Him can be found,
and if we look for them, they will surely astound.

Each Christmas no matter how busy we get,
Let's stop for a moment and take time to reflect,
On a very old saying I've found to be true,
With my very best wishes I'll share it with you -

Wise Men still seek Jesus!

The wise men's visit is recorded in **Matthew's Gospel, chapter 2:11-12.**

Nativity and After... Fulfilment of Promise.

*Christmas with all its excitement and traditions is over in a flash. The day comes and goes, and for children it seems like ages till it comes around. We all know the Nativity Story and for many the images on our cards of the baby in the stable come and go from our minds just as quickly. There is more to the Nativity story than the baby, angels, shepherds and wise men. They are all part of a much bigger plan. A man called Simeon found this out when he met the baby Jesus soon after His birth. Simeon doesn't get a mention in the Christmas story much, but he has an important role. His story is found in the book of **Luke Chapter 2 verses 25-35**.*

"For years I had waited – Messiah **would** come,
I knew God had promised I'd see His Chosen One.
I went to the Temple each day just to pray,
and to listen and learn of all God had to say.

One day, in my heart I heard God whisper to me,
'Go now to the Temple and today you will see.'
I went, my heart pounding – my life's dream would unfold.
And I knew when God spoke to do as I was told.

The courtyard was crowded, the Temple so busy,
Afraid I would miss Him, I was all of a tizzy.
The voice spoke again, 'Simeon, look over there.'
So I lifted my eyes and could not help but stare.

I saw a poor couple with their baby son.
Was this the Messiah – could He be the One?
I spoke to the parents and then held the boy
they told me their story, I now wept with joy.

They told me of shepherds and angels; a stable.
Had I not heard God's voice, I'd have thought it a fable.
But I knew as I held this child, born to be King,
He would grow to do mighty works, change everything.

God kept His promise, though I did not expect
to see such a wee baby, I had no regret.
I had learned I could trust whatever God said,
even though other thoughts danced in my head."

Messiah **had** come, He was born Son of Man,
and the path He would follow was his Father's plan.
Like Simeon we too have our plans, hopes, a dream,
that don't always work out – or so it would seem.

The Nativity story reminds us each year,
that God knows what He's doing – we have no need to fear.
In each New Year that follows, let's trust and not doubt,
God knows all about us and all will work out.

Anna rejoices…

Ok. This isn't a typical Christmas poem but it does tell part of the Nativity story. The infant Jesus appeared to the most unlikely of people in the most unlikely way and the most unlikely places. Anna was one of those people. She was an old lady whose life didn't seem to adhere to convention. But she saw the fulfilment of what she hoped for because of Jesus' birth. That's what Christmas is about. Who says life has to adhere to convention?
Find the story in Luke 2: verses 36-38.

"I had many plans as a very young wife,
for my husband and I - what we'd do with our life.
Yet I was a widow in seven short years,
with no children either and I shed many tears.
But I made a decision then – I would trust God,
And allow Him to choose the path I now trod.

So it has been since that very first day,
I go now to God's house to give praise and to pray.
He promised a Saviour, through the prophets foretold,
and I'm waiting for Him, even though I'm now old.
God's plans are the best in the long run I know,
now what He's revealed has just proven it so.

Today at the Temple I heard Simeon gasp,
for he said he had seen the Messiah at last.
I too saw the couple with their baby Son,
And I knew in my heart that this Child was the One.
Who had come to the world to deliver us all –
both the rich and the poor, with the great and the small.

Heard His parents recall how His birth came about;
Such miraculous things I'd no reason to doubt.
The star and the shepherds, the wise men as well,
I resolved there and then many others to tell

Of the child I have seen - the Messiah has come,
and although I am old my work's not yet done.

For the rest of my days I want always to tell,
That God kept His promise and all will be well"

And so at this time if you feel a bit jaded,
For you all the sparkle of Christmas has faded,
The promise revealed then to Anna still true,
And it can be found now by both me and you.
In the forthcoming year if your plans go awry,
Then you may get angry, you might even cry.

Take a lesson from Anna, on misfortune don't dwell.
God still keeps His promises, all will be well.

Zebedee is deserted

My sons and I were fishermen,
as my father was before.
We earned our living casting nets
Just off the Galilee shore.

Sometimes we'd catch a-plenty,
and others none at all.
That all changed when John and James
followed a new teacher's call.

Jesus came from Nazareth,
we knew His family well.
Yet there was something special
about Him, we could tell.

You see, Simon our partner went fishing
one night, and at that time caught naught.
Next day Jesus asked could He borrow the boat
and from it a great crowd He taught.

When Jesus had finished His teaching
He turned then to Simon to say,
"Go out once more and then cast out your nets,"
How could he catch fish? – It was day.

But the nets, well they filled full to bursting,
and we had to help haul them all in.
Simon fell on his knees before Jesus,
he was now so aware of his sin.

Jesus told him he wouldn't be fishing
out on the sea anymore.
He said He would make him a fisher of men,
a call Simon just could not ignore.

My boys felt they had to go with Him,
turning their backs on the sea.
They couldn't tell what lay before them
when they left boat and nets just with me.

Over the next years I watched them,
I knew they were never the same.
And all because they had met Jesus,
and believed in the power of His name.

Zebedee's story reminds us
the message the same now as then.
even today Jesus calls us –
He's still needing fishers of men.

The calling of James and John is found in the **Gospel of Mark, chapter 1: 19-20**, and Peter's catch of fish in **Luke's Gospel, chapter 5: 1-11**.

Just five loaves and a couple of fish

"The Rabbi from Nazareth's coming!" they said
I was excited, thoughts a-whirl in my head.
I wanted to see Him and all of a tizzy,
for my father was working, my mother was busy.
But she gave me her blessing and said with a smile,
"You'd best take some food, for you may be a while."
She packed five barley loaves and a couple of fish,
said, "Go learn from this Jesus if that's what you wish."

A large crowd had gathered – there were 5000 men,
plus the women and children, let's not forget them.
We listened intently; the time went so fast,
though it seemed a short while, many hours had passed.
Jesus stopped speaking, then some heard Him say,
"We must feed these people, not send them away."
His followers though seemed unsure what He meant,
but to the midst of the crowd they were each of them sent.

The one they called Andrew approached where I sat,
and he looked like he didn't know what to be at.
Hesitantly he asked, "Do you have any food?"
"Would my loaves and fishes be of any good?"
I heard myself stutter; though inside I thought
"Not many can share the wee drop that I've brought."
Then Andrew and I made our way through the crowd.
"What will Jesus do now?" I wondered aloud.

My heart was fast pounding and all of a flutter,
"Here's five loaves and two fish" I heard Andrew mutter.
Jesus took them and nodded without any fuss,
Then He held them aloft right in front of us.
"Father," He said, "Will You now bless what's given."
As He lifted His face with a smile towards Heaven.
He gave food to His followers, said – "Pass it round",
then He bade all who watched to sit down on the ground.

The disciples indeed passed it round everyone,
and my eyes shone with wonder at what He had done.
He'd prayed very simply, I'd heard what He said,
but now all who had gathered had been fully fed.
So on going home at the end of the day,
I knew I would always follow His way.
My youth and my offering Jesus did not despise,
and I learned a lesson and now realised -

That the food that I brought, well, it had filled a hole,
But the words Jesus spoke, they were food for my soul.

The feeding of the 5000 can be found in the Gospel of John, chapter 6: 1-14.

The Bridegroom comes

Caught in the act; guilty as charged,
no hope of anything but a quick death.
Free from the pain caused by the boulders that
would bring about my end.
Free from the pain of the sin that left me exposed,
in front of those considered more righteous than I.

I did not look at His face
till He knelt and met my eye.
Considering their question about my fate,
He wrote slowly in the sand.
Never dropping His eyes, He said,
"Let him without sin cast the first stone."

It had grown quiet with expectation,
so His voice echoed in the courtyard.
One by one I heard the thud of rocks hitting the ground.
Silence fell once more, then He spoke again.
"Where are your accusers? None condemn and nor do I".

He lifted me up, still watching.
I realised what He had done, and the debt I owed;
the protection and forgiveness that had been
afforded to me.
"Go," He said, "and sin no more."
I went; confident in the knowledge that
I would see Him again...

...For the Bridegroom will come for His Bride.

The un-named woman's encounter with Jesus is recorded in the Gospel of **John, chapter 8: 1-11.**

Belovèd Zacchaeus

I am not liked.
I steal money; I am a tax collector.
Rome gets its due, but I do too.
I am small in people's eyes – physically and in standing.
I am nothing.

I see the looks and hear the whispers,
the extra shekels hide my loneliness.
I throw wild parties and people come,
but only to eat, drink and be merry.
Not to be my friend.

I hear the stories.
Nice that someone else has grabbed the attention of the gossips.
Jesus works miracles they say;
Blind men see and lame men walk.
He's coming here. Everyone wants to see – even me!

The streets are crowded.
No one gives an inch – what do they owe me?
But somehow the desire to see Him overcomes my disappointment.
I will make a way,
even if I have to climb this tree.

He's coming this way.
Not much to look at, yet He has such peace on His face.
What's that – He knows I'm here? He speaks my very name.
To eat with me, He says, at my home,
He wants to come.

He came. I was not sure He would.
He spoke and I heard life in His words.
He came to heal hurts, in hearts as well as bodies.
He healed me and I am changed.
I am a new man.

I will give back what I owe.
The money is not important now.
My stature and standing have not changed.
But I have. Jesus made a difference.
He came for me and I know now I am loved.

Zacchaeus' story can be found **in Luke's Gospel, chapter 19: 1-10.**

They say that a leopard can change its spots, but an encounter with Jesus can change the hardest of hearts.

Living Water

<u>11am</u>
I go to the well at the height of the day,
that way I know there will be no one else in my way.
I won't have to pretend I don't notice
the whispers and rejection which cut me to the quick.
Although I would **never** let those other women know.

As a child I wanted the same things they have,
A home, someone to love and a family.
But I made some wrong choices and some were made for me,
which means I'm now an outcast.
This was **never** what I wanted.

I'm not sure how much longer I can wear the mask of indifference,
when all I really want is acceptance.
After all, they too have made mistakes, just different ones from mine.
I long for that as a parched throat longs for a cold drink.
But I can't change who I am, so that's **never** likely to be offered.

Noon
The man sitting at the well didn't move when I approached.
I really wanted to run, but I needed the water.
He asked for a drink and there was no threat in his voice.
I couldn't hide my surprise and said so,
but **never** expected His reply.

He promised water that would quench my thirst.
He knew all about me; everything!
Yet I felt no condemnation, only hope.
He told me who He was and I believed Him.
He said I would **never** thirst again.

12.30pm
I felt clean inside, and this time I did run.
Back into town, laughing and shouting as I did.
Come and meet the Man who told me all about myself!
I'm not sure who was most surprised.
I **never** expected them to follow but they did.

2 Days later
He stayed a few days and everyone saw it was true,
I was not the only one who changed.
Sins that others had hidden were exposed,
and forgiven - just like mine.
We drank from the water of life and were **never** the same.

The Samaritan woman's testimony is found in the **Gospel of John, chapter 4: verses 1-42.** It reminds us that no-one is perfect (except Jesus) but we can all be changed – though not in our own strength. And we should not be quick to judge.

'But the Pharisees and their scribes complained to Jesus' disciples, "Why do you eat and drink with tax collectors and sinners?" **Jesus answered, "It is not the healthy who need a doctor, but the sick.** *I have not come to call the righteous, but sinners, to repentance.'* **Luke 5:30-31.**

Bartimaeus gets his heart's desire

I sat most days at the city gate to beg a coin or two.
Although I could not see, I heard most every point of view,
for the people who passed through the gate, they talked and shared their news.
If what I heard that day was true, I had no time to lose.

Jesus of Nazareth was here, so they said,
and the things I heard of him spun round in my head.
They said He did miracles - healings and such,
that He changed people's lives with just one simple touch.

He was coming my way, for I heard the commotion,
but to get His attention I had not a notion
of how I could get Him to stop by my side,
so, I took a deep breath and I cast out my pride.

I shouted so loud in the midst of the riot,
that some folks just jeered and told me to be quiet.
Others said that He'd stopped and had asked me to come -
"Cheer up Bartimaeus, now don't be so glum!"

His voice clear and calm, and my heart how it pounded,
but what happened next left the crowd all astounded.
He asked very tenderly, "What can I do?"
I replied, "Teacher, I want to see You!"

He told me because of my faith I was healed,
and my eyes filled with wonder as all was revealed.
For I saw Him indeed; from my darkness now free.
Jesus had truly done that for me.

He set off again with his friends, down the road,
My heart was so full and my face it just glowed.
I decided to follow, no reason to stay -
I wanted to learn from Him all of my days.

If I had kept quiet things would still be the same,
I'm so glad I was bold, and I called out His name.
I've vowed to tell others to call on Him too –
If He did this for me, what will He do for you?

Bartimaeus' healing is recorded in **Mark's Gospel, chapter 10: 46 - 52**.

Sometimes we have to step out in faith, even if to others it seems foolish and they try to put us off.

Jairus' hope is tested

The crowds were waiting for His arrival,
full of expectant hope.
I was desperate, and fell at His feet
as the other leaders frowned at my lack of propriety.

For Tikvah* my little hope, my joy; fast fading,
Jesus was her only hope.
 He said that He would come,
so we pushed through the crowds.

I wanted to run home, but Jesus stopped.
"Who touched me?" He asked.
I didn't care, as long as He touched my girl,
but He waited.

A woman came forward, trembling,
and told her story.
Sick for as long as my girl has been alive,
and now healed.

Jesus called her 'daughter' and smiled at her faith.
My daughter needed Him too - we had to go.
When my servant arrived I knew then all hope was lost.
Yet He told me to have faith; like the woman.

At the house the mourners wailed,
but they laughed when He said she just slept.
I took my wife's hand and we followed Him with his friends.
However, the commotion stopped as He'd bid.

Our little girl lay still and pale - what could He do?
He took her hand and spoke without fuss.
"Get up, my child."
Jesus was smiling again.

In an instant, Tikvah did as He asked,
and He passed her to her mother's embrace.
As the colour returned to her cheeks Jesus looked at me
and nodded as the tears streamed down mine.

I could not find my voice.
Here stood my child, our little 'hope'.
Here too stood the Christ -
eternal hope in the face of death.

The raising of Jairus' daughter is recorded in **Luke's Gospel, chapter 8: 40-56.**

*Tikvah is a popular Jewish girl's name. It is the Hebrew word for hope.

Lazarus, Come Forth...

Sick and fevered, tossing turning,
sisters anxious. Is He coming?
Time is passing, life is ebbing,
but it's too late; now tears they're shedding.
It seems death's won.

Christ comes unhurried, with a purpose,
says, "Don't worry or be anxious".
Believe in Him and see His glory,
Soon they'll see a different story.
What will He do?

Jesus goes to His friend's grave,
But why go now – too late to save?
The mourners know great things He's done,
Why the delay to heal this one -
did He not care?

A crowd is gathered and expectant;
Anticipation is infectant.
They see Him weep when He draws near,
they've never seen Him shed a tear.
See how He loved him.

"Now take away the stone", He says,
and they all watch it done, amazed;
The Word speaks three, Lazarus obeys,
The crowd cannot avert their gaze –
their friend from death now freed.

And so indeed, Christ loved His friend,
but this is not the story's end.
For only just a few weeks later,
Jesus then did something greater -
that changed the world.

He too within a tomb was laid,
the sacrifice for sin He'd paid.
When He arose up from **that** grave,
He freed the world He'd come to save
from Satan's power.

Christ loves us all.

Read about the raising of Lazarus in the Gospel of **John, chapter 11: 1-42.**

A song on Palm Sunday

On borrowed colt, down Olivet,
Christ rode in from the east,
like others to Jerusalem
for the Passover feast.
Some had seen the wonders,
others still had heard the stories,
 and so, they came to welcome Him
and they sang His praise and glory.

"Hosanna to King David's Son"
was their resounding cry;
Yet He hadn't come to claim a crown,
but on a cross to die.
Their joy and adoration
too soon would pass away.
It would disappear like sunset
at the closing of the day.

He knew men's hearts; He wept for them
as He approached the City gates.
In days those cheers and shouts would turn
to anger, jeers and hate.
They thought Jesus would free them
from their captors of the day,
He'd come indeed to set them free,
but in a different way.

He said later, "Peace I leave you,"
meaning peace of mind and heart,
with the promise of forgiveness
and in life a brand-new start.
Jesus never sought to compromise -
He taught them wrong from right.
He lived life to the fullest
and did so with all his might.

He trusted in His Father
doing everything He asked,
though the path He trod was daunting;
He'd been set an awesome task.
On the cross He cried, "It's finished,"
for that task was now complete.
He'd done all that was required of Him,
and never known defeat.

After three days in a garden tomb,
He came back to life once more.
And He promised we'd do greater things
than He had done before.
If we'd learn to love and trust Him,
begin walking that same road,
then He promised He'd walk with us,
and He'd share our heavy load.

Like the crowds on that Palm Sunday,
our faith can waver too.
But if we turn out hearts to Him,
He'll show us what to do.
He'll be with us as He promised;
If we seek Him He'll be found.
If we give Him opportunity,
He'll turn our lives around.

Luke 19:41-44 . As he approached Jerusalem and saw the city, he wept over it and said, "If you, even you, had only known on this day what would bring you peace—but now it is hidden from your eyes. The days will come upon you when your enemies will build an embankment against you and encircle you and hem you in on every side. They will dash you to the ground, you and the children within your walls. They will not leave one stone on another, because you did not recognize the time of God's coming to you."

Never think the things that make us weep don't affect Jesus. He knows the wickedness of the heart and weeps over it.

Malchus recalls

'I work for Caiaphas – he's the high priest.
But I'm just his servant - one of the least.
When he needed a spy though he made me his ear,
sent me out and about – said "Report what you hear,
of Jesus the Nazarene and all that you see,
and then come back quickly, tell all to me."

So, I watched and I listened, but did not understand
just why my master did not like this man.
Jesus taught that to lead you must first be a slave,
He came not to condemn, but to seek and to save.
His words somehow stuck as I listened for more,
and to follow Him round was no longer a chore.

I reported with joy all I'd heard and I'd found,
And Caiaphas faithfully noted it down.
But I found myself hoping that all would be well,
that he'd finally believe all the things I would tell.
Of the miracles - good things for this Christ was no threat,
I hoped that His teaching would reach Caiaphas yet.

Then suddenly things took a sinister twist,
And I never thought I would be party to this.
To Jesus' arrest I was ordered to follow,
up to Gethsemane, into the hollow.
The Teacher was there, and His followers too,
He did not try to hide - He was seen in plain view.

But one of the followers, Judas his name,
At the head of the crowd gave a sign as we came.
He greeted his friend with a word and a kiss,
which I could not believe - Oh what treachery this!
A commotion arose, swords were drawn, voices raised,
And what happened next is a bit of a haze.

Oh, I knew I was struck; saw the blood, felt the pain,
and I feared that my life would no more be the same.
But then Jesus rebuked them and banished my fear,
for He touched me, spoke simply and restored my ear.
I watched all unfold later, saw Him mocked, watched Him die.
"Don't you know what you're doing?" I wanted to cry.

This Man gave Himself, spoke of love, spoke the truth -
We should be proclaiming His words from the roof!
As he breathed his last He said, – "Father forgive,"
And I knew that's the way that I wanted to live.
But after his death I thought that was the end –
That I'd no longer follow, or be His friend.

I went back to Caiaphas, sad and bereft,
Unsure and uncertain – what hope had I left?
And then three days later, something had changed;
Caiaphas was furious, as one deranged -
The soldiers reported the body had gone,
And the stone rolled away at the first light of dawn.

I then remembered what Jesus had said,
"In three days I will rise," - **He was no longer dead!**
My broken heart leapt and I knew it was true,
though my master it seemed did not know what to do.
But I smiled to myself; the news filled me with glee,
I knew Jesus had risen and loved even me!'

And like Malchus that slave, we can also believe,
that no matter our past we too have a reprieve.
Jesus died, not just for Malchus; He died for us too.
and not only for Caiaphas, but me and you.
I hope you'll accept the good news that I tell -
Christ has indeed risen and all can be well.

The account of what happened to Malchus is found in the Gospels of:
Matthew - Chapter 26 verses 47 to 56; **Mark** – Chapter 14, verses 46 to 48; **Luke** -Chapter 22, verses 47 to 53; **John** – Chapter 18, verses 1 to 11.

Barabbas is pardoned...

"I always was a rebel
and I hated Roman rule.
Those who longed to live in peace -
I thought they were just fools.
I fought hard and I battled;
for a bounty I was sought.
I held out for a little while,
till I was finally caught.

I knew what fate awaited me
as I languished in that cell.
I would hang upon a Roman cross,
and I'd suffer utter hell.
I had no hope of pardon,
for my list of crimes was long.
and I knew that I'd be punished
for the things that I'd done wrong.

I was told a mob had gathered
to see who would be set free.
They yelled, "Give us Barabbas"
but why should they ask for me?
I'd done nothing to deserve it;
And Pilate knew that too.
But it was a Roman custom,
there was nothing he could do.

Shocked and a bit bewildered,
I was told that I could go.
Perhaps I was just dreaming –
or was it really so?
I watched; silent as they flogged Him,
and I winced at every blow.
Why had He become my substitute?
I was desperate to know.

His body bruised and bloodied,
Jesus staggered through the streets,
and I was drawn to follow,
amidst all the noise and heat.
But He didn't look defeated,
That's not how He seemed to me,
I was the one loosed from my chains,
Yet He was truly free.

I heard Jesus cry, "It's finished"
then I heard the soldier say,
'This Man was the Son of God'
and I sadly went my way.
Some of the crowd shared stories
of the things Jesus had done,
they had believed He truly was
God's Holy, Chosen Son.

For the next two days I wondered
whether I could really change.
To ensure that Jesus' sacrifice
had not been made in vain.
Early that third morning
I headed out to pray,
perhaps God would forgive me;
I was not sure what to say.

I saw some women running -
I had seen them at the cross.
So why now were they laughing
when they'd suffered such a loss?
I asked them, why so happy?
and they looked at me and said
that they had just met Jesus,
for He was no longer dead.

Then a gentle peace enveloped me,
and I fell down on my knees,
I offered my life back to God
to do with as He pleased.
I knew now I was forgiven,
because Jesus took my place.
And one day I'll thank Him properly
When I see Him face to face. "

Like Barabbas we can mess things up,
we might think that it's too late,
To turn around and start again,
Forgetting fear or hate.
The point of the Easter story
Is that Jesus took _our_ place.
We can start afresh because of this,
And that, my friends, is Grace.

Find Barabbas' story in the Gospel of **Mark, Chapter 15, verses 6-15.**

Pilate's dilemma

'I am used to men pleading; they will do what I say;
If it saves their own skin at the end of the day.
The priests – well they normally stay well away,
except that weekend they had plenty to say.

He was beaten already but ever so calm,
and appearing before me He showed no alarm.
I heard all the stories now could it be true?
So I asked, "Are you really the King of the Jews?"

I had heard the reports from the Sunday before,
and of miracles done along Galilee's shore.
He now stood before me and so could it be
that one of His miracles I'd get to see.

But He lifted His eyes and I knew He could see
all of my thoughts – He knew all about me!
I who had power to kill or set free,
yet I knew this Man Jesus had power over me.

My wife even warned me to leave Him alone -
to sit not in judgement on Governor's throne.
But the crowds were all shouting that He had to die,
"Do not release Him", they cried. "Crucify!"

Swept along by the moment I listened in fear,
and I first had Him flogged - even that raised a cheer.
My conscience had told me He'd done nothing wrong.
but to save **my** own skin I was carried along.

Now I felt the fear like those others had known,
in the midst of the vast crowd I felt so alone.
But I still washed my hands and sent Him to a cross,
and yet it was me who felt sorrow and loss.

Then three days later the priests came once more;
The body had gone there was such a furore.
Could it truly have been that it was just as He'd said?
He was really the Christ and was no longer dead.'

And Jesus had risen, it really was true –
He offered Himself to save both me and you.
He knows all about us and does not condemn,
His hand reaches out for he wants to befriend.

Pilate did many things he could regret,
And we may have likewise and even more yet.
But because of God's love we can cast those away,
And rejoice with our Christ on each new Easter day.

Read of Jesus before Pilate in the Gospel of **Matthew, chapter 27, verses 11-26.**

It's easy to go with the majority when we are afraid of taking a stand, but sometimes we just have to do what we know to be right, or we will live to regret our actions.

1 Peter 3:14:"[14] But even if you should suffer for what is right, you are blessed Do not fear their threats[a]; do not be frightened."

Simon's story

'When I finally reached Jerusalem, my heart was really glad.
But once within the city gates, what I found there made me sad,
for I saw a mob of people who had gathered in the streets,
some were mocking, some were jeering, others still could only weep.

Roman soldiers led three prisoners towards the city wall,
but one of them was struggling, and then I saw Him fall.
He was beaten and exhausted, and I knew not what His crime,
but then, just for a second, His eyes looked into mine.

For you see a soldier grabbed me,
barked, "pick up His cross and walk."
Now I was also midst the crowd, and I could hear their talk.
"You cannot kill this Man," one cried, "He raised me up for I had died."
"And I can see," another said – "He put new eyes within my head."

We finally reached the place; the soldiers hung three crosses high,
I found I could not turn away, so I stayed to watch Him die.
I heard He was a teacher who'd shown people how to live,
Not 'eye for eye' or 'tooth for tooth', but 'love your enemy, forgive.'

His followers, it seemed, afraid, had mostly run away.
But there was something in His presence that
compelled me still to stay.
He cried out, "It is finished", and the soldier standing by
said he knew this was the Son of God, then finally **I** cried.

I didn't fully understand, perhaps only in part,
that the One who died upon that cross, knew the blackness of **my** heart.
No longer clean for Passover, I could not yet go home,
so I stayed a while longer, just with my thoughts alone.

I found out more about this man and wished I'd known Him well.
Nearly everyone I spoke to had a story they could tell,
of how their lives had changed since they'd spent time with Him,
and how they knew that now they'd been forgiven of their sin.

And so, upon the third day, I thought perhaps that I should leave,
but then I met some women who'd gone to His tomb to grieve.
When they got there it was empty - met an angel too they said,
who had told them Christ was risen, that He was no longer dead.

They went on their way rejoicing, and somehow, I did too,
For although it seemed impossible, within my heart I knew,
that the Man whose cross I'd carried knew my deepest thoughts within,
And finally, I knew that I could ask forgiveness for my sin.

Though the time spent in Jerusalem was not what I had thought,
I wouldn't change one moment for the peace and joy it brought.
And returning to Cyrene, I had so much to tell,
of all I had experienced; in my heart all was now well.'

Simon's story shows us though our plans may not work out,
That there's someone we can trust, who knows what we are all about.
From Christ there are no secrets, and He loves us just the same,
Just remember that at Easter - 'twas for us too that He came.

The story of Simon of Cyrene can be found **in Luke's Gospel, chapter 23: 26 to 33.**

An Arimathean Miracle – Joseph finds his courage.

"For months I heard the stories of how Jesus healed the sick,
I even watched Him from a distance, and I saw this was no trick.
I heard Him teach that God is love and it's better to forgive.
To leave the past, move forward; that's the way, He said, to live.

For years I studied scripture, prayed Messiah soon would come.
Now really, was it possible that Jesus was the One?
I had power and authority, gained over many years,
to give them up and follow him - I had so many fears.

People would scoff and laugh perhaps, and then what would I say?
Although I felt with all my heart He was showing us the way.
And so I followed from afar; in secret – no one knew,
but then something awful happened and I knew what I must do.

You see they crucified Him, as a criminal on a cross,
His mother and disciples, how they suffered – all was lost.
The Sabbath was approaching and they couldn't leave Him there.
But what happened next amazed me and made folks I knew just stare.

For you see I went to Pilate, asked to take the body down.
and said I was a follower - and yes, I saw him frown.
When Jesus lived I was a coward and I hid what I believed,
but now I had to stand up and no longer be deceived.

I took my stand; we carried Him into the tomb I'd made.
I took with me Nicodemus who had also been afraid.
Then I waited with the others, filled with sorrow - what a mess!
If I'd spoken up for Jesus, would they have punished him much less?

That Sunday morning, women left to anoint Him in His tomb.
I watched them as they set off, my heart heavy still with gloom.
But then they came back running, they had seen Him so they said.
they told us that He had risen - that He was no longer dead.

That seemed so hard to take in; could it be really true?
My mind was in a quandary, I did not know what to do.
We were hiding from authorities what they'd do no one could tell,
but as we sat there trembling, He appeared to us as well.

'Fear not,' He told us, 'I am here - and I will always be,'
And in my heart I knew He had included even me."
Still Jesus' words apply today to all who suffer fear,
for He has never left us - when we ask Him, He comes near.

Joseph's story can be found in **Mark 15: 43 -46;**
Luke 23: 50-56 and 19: 38.

Jesus will use even cowards who are willing.

The Centurion's story

He was a faithful soldier, loyal to his country's throne.
He was a man of some authority, yet he often felt alone.
He was living in a foreign land, didn't understand their way,
but he had to follow orders and he knew he had to stay.
He had unpleasant duties, and he had to watch folk die,
not allowed to show emotion as he watched their families cry.
Today it was no different, standing guard beneath a cross,
another family weeping, devastated by their loss.

Yet, somehow, he was troubled; something really wasn't right,
for it seemed a King was hanging there, it was a fearsome sight.
He'd heard the tales from Galilee of all this Man had done,
the blind could see, the lame could walk, and some said He was God's Son.
The Man had done no wrong it seemed, and yet why was He here?
Even Pilate tried to free Him, but he'd heard the people jeer.
This Man who'd done so many things, for a world full of strife,
not only had the sick been healed, but a man brought back to life.

And now, where were His followers? - The soldier saw but one,
the other men deserted Him, in spite of all He'd done.
The Man somehow was not bitter as He hung
there in the heat.
And the soldier could sense victory, when there should have been defeat.
And whilst his own men gambled, casting lots for this Man's coat,
the soldier saw folk stop to watch and others mock and gloat.
Then something awesome happened as the sky grew dark and black.
The soldier wondered would God come - was He ready to attack?

But in a final, loud voice the Man cried 'Father forgive.'
And then the soldier realised he'd been shown how to live.
Though as yet he didn't fully understand, somehow he knew this **WAS** God's Son,
and he declared this boldly, there in front of everyone.
We know nothing more about him; we don't even know his name.
And yet I'm sure this soldier's life was never quite the same.

For you see he had met Jesus, like the others, he now knew
that he had to turn his life around, Christ had shown him what to do.
To live his life as an example, never more to hold a grudge
on the circumstance he found himself, and of others not to judge.
And his story still reminds us, Jesus came that **ALL** might live,
It wasn't just the crowds that Friday for whom Christ cried 'forgive.'
And so once again at Easter will you join in thanks with me,
For everything that Jesus did so we could all be free.

Read about the centurion in **Luke 23:32-47.**

What Cleopas learned on the road to Emmaus...

'Why stay in Jerusalem after Jesus had been killed?
Now it seemed that all our hopes and dreams could never be fulfilled.
After everything we'd been through I just wanted to go home,
and a good friend travelled with me so I wouldn't be alone.

We trudged along the road that day, so weary, to Emmaus,
talking over all that happened; our minds were all in chaos.
A 'stranger' came upon us then and joined us on our way,
He listened quite intently to all we had to say.

We told Him about Jesus and the miracles He'd done,
and for a while how we had thought He was the Chosen One.
Until that Friday on a cross He had been hung to die;
the Pharisees so keen to prove His teaching all a lie.

But on that Sunday morning, in the midst of all the gloom,
some women to the graveside went and found an empty tomb.
"You foolish men," the 'stranger' said, **"Did you not understand?
Though everything seems dark to you, God has it all in hand."**

He taught us from the scriptures then, our hearts began to burn,
and we finally reached Emmaus at the setting of the sun.
He made to go on further, but we both bade Him stay,
and join us in our evening meal, for we sensed He'd more to say.

As we sat there at the table, He arose to bless the meal,
and then what happened next to us seemed really quite surreal.
He raised His arms in blessing, with the nail marks now in view,
and though He disappeared just then, we knew that it was true.

Jesus surely had arisen, just as the women said,
For He really had spent time with us – He was no longer dead.
We had to tell the others, although it was now late,
so we set off for Jerusalem at quite a hasty rate.

We told our friends what Jesus said, - How God had all things planned,
when suddenly in front of us, the Lord Himself did stand.
We didn't fully understand, but we trusted just the same,
when He told us He would send us out to do work in His name.'

It was as Jesus told them, right at the very start,
and His Spirit travelled with them, changing many heavy hearts.
What they all learned that weekend, is just as true today,
when things seem at their bleakest, that's when God will have His way.

His plans and purposes for us we may not yet understand,
but can trust like the disciples that He has everything in hand.

Cleopas' story can be found in **Luke Chapter 24, verses 13-53.**

Peter finds forgiveness

"To Jerusalem He said we'd go,
it was a sacred time.
He'd set His face quite resolute
upon a path divine.
He knew He would be crucified,
He told us so, you see,
But this seemed quite ridiculous;
- Impossible to me.

I had left my livelihood
to follow after Him,
seen Jesus working miracles,
forgive people for their sins.
He healed the sick, the lame could walk,
thousands more than once were fed.
But yes, in spite of all of this,
some folks did want Him dead.

I often speak before I think –
can't seem to let things lie,
I was aghast when Jesus told me though
three times I'd Him deny.
I vowed I would protect Him,
I am often brash and bold.
But it was true, I let Him down,
I did as I'd been told.

I let my fears condemn us both,
It tore my heart in two.
The day Jesus was crucified,
I did not know what to do.
On that third day when first we heard
about the empty tomb,
with Angels waiting at its door
amidst the morning gloom .

The women, well they met Him first,
but John and I ran on.
T'was true the grave was empty,
and I wondered where He'd gone.
But then once more I was afraid,
as I thought of what I'd done.
How badly I'd let down my friend,
And God's belovèd Son.

But then another miracle,
for Jesus came to me.
He told me He forgave me,
that He died to set me free
from all my pride and foolishness,
I would leave those things behind.
He wanted me to speak for Him –
Go out to all mankind."

You see Peter, he was just like us,
we do things that we regret.
But like him please remember,
Christ forgives us even yet.
Every Easter Peter's story
reminds us of what's true,
there are always new beginnings –

Jesus died for me and you.

John chapter 21: 12-19. *Jesus repeated the question: "Simon son of John, do you love me?" "Yes, Lord," Peter said, "you know I love you." "Then take care of my sheep," Jesus said.*

I picture Peter the disciple as always plunging into situations, sometimes without thinking. Some people refer to him as 'the big fisherman'. His heart, however, was always in the right place. Ultimately when circumstances got too difficult for him, he crumbled – but then so can we.

And in his forgiveness and restoration at Easter there is hope for us too!

PART TWO – ENJOY THE JOURNEY

Valentine's Day

Red roses and other bouquets displayed in cellophane
declare undying love at a price far more than their value.

They will prove, if only for a short time,
that the recipient is worthy of the cost.

But when they are gone who will remember
the price that was paid?

And yet, everlasting love died,
displayed upon an ugly cross.

No flowers, only thorns,
but their message still remains.

His 'I love you' was not for a season,
so priceless that it came as a gift.

An eternal valentine offered to any
who is willing to receive it.

The giver of the gift still feels
That we are worthy of the cost.

John 15:13. *"*Greater love has no one than this: to lay down one's life for one's friends.*"*

Once

This land knew you once, Lord,
In a deep and holy way.
The people knew you once, Lord,
came before you for each day.

This used to be a holy land
when the people followed you.
They trusted you for everything,
let you show them what to do.

But that was once, some time ago.
Now the holy light's gone dim.
The people go their own way now –
the land's dying, lost in sin.

There were people, once, who lived here,
and whose hearts you set aflame,
so that everything they said or did
brought glory to your name.

Though they no longer live here now,
they are living now with you,
and there's still lives here who praise you, Lord.
Burn the fire now anew.

This was a land that knew you, once,
let it know you, Lord, again.
Show us how to live by faith,
let us cause you no more pain.

We must cherish our inheritance,
it is a precious thing.
In this land soon, let's once again
crown you our Lord and King.

2 Chronicles 7:14. "If my people, who are called by my name, will humble themselves and pray and seek my face and turn from their wicked ways, then I will hear from heaven, and I will forgive their sin and will heal their land. "

As a wee girl, I remember being taught bible stories by my Grandpa Murphy who took it for granted that this should be part of my upbringing. He enjoyed reading them to me as much as I enjoyed learning. However, I am sure many families don't see that as part of everyday life now. Thankfully, the promise in 2 Chronicles still applies because God is still the same today as He was then.

When the Sparrow Falls.

A single sparrow's fallen,
but does anybody care?
It was special, now it's fallen,
and we pass by unaware.

Or we stop – just for a moment,
Shake our heads and then move on.
We **are** sorry that it's fallen,
but it's too late now, it's gone.

Yet God weeps for that one sparrow,
As He grieves for each life lost.
For He made a way to save them,
And He paid the highest cost.

And for each life now that's purchased
by the blood of God's dear Son,
He expects us all to care,
and share His love with everyone.

We must learn to love each sparrow,
Try to show it where to fly.
For it may just be a sparrow,
But it's special in God's eyes.

Matthew 10:29: *"Are not two sparrows sold for a penny? Yet not one of them will fall to the ground outside your Father's care."*

I wrote this in the year that my brother's childhood hero, Davie Cooper died, and my cousin George Broadfoot, a few months later. For whether we are heroes, or the boy next door, we are all loved – that's why Christ died.

In every Wilderness.

In every wilderness there is a path –
well worn, for it is the only
safe way to pass through.
And many have come this way before,
or will follow on behind.
In this place provision will be found
for the weary traveller,
But often in unexpected places;
A spring of water to refresh the weary soul
before it continues its journey.

In every wilderness there is a guide –
One who knows the way already,
who will point out both the pitfalls
and the rugged beauty of the desert.
A beauty that is not man made,
where it is possible, but only
by following the Guide's implicit instruction,
for a traveller to enjoy this experience.

In every wilderness the joy
of passing through and coming out,
Is surpassed only by the gratitude
that there has never been a time
where the pilgrim has been alone
in the desert,
or else they would never have made it.

Inspired by the book written by Jamie Buckingham, "A Way through the Wilderness," *
where he describes a trek through the Sinai desert.

Isaiah 43:19: "See, I am doing a new thing! Now it springs up; do you not perceive it? I am making a way in the wilderness and streams in the wasteland."

Thank God, we are never alone - even in the desert places!

*" A Way Through the Wilderness" by Jamie Buckingham. Copyright © 2013 Risky Living Ministries Inc. Original Publication 1983.

The Storm - Walking on Water

When the storm breaks do you run for cover?
Trying to hide from its wrath.
Or, taking a deep breath
do you launch out into the waves?
Trusting the One
who will not let them bring you down to death.

For though they roar about your tiny vessel,
filling your ears with noise and cries of fear,
in the midst of the storm there is still peace –
For the Giver of peace is there, waiting;
In the eye of the storm.

And there you will find
that the waves cannot harm you.
Though looking around you may think
that you have done a foolish thing,
as the waves rise up, mockingly, to meet you.

But you do not drown,
for loving arms reach out to keep you up.
And gentle eyes reprove,
but don't condemn.
Then suddenly…
The storm is over and the sun is shining upon you.

Romans 8:38-39: "[38] For I am convinced that neither death nor life, neither angels nor demons,[k] neither the present nor the future, nor any powers, [39] neither height nor depth, nor anything else in all creation, will be able to separate us from the love of God that is in Christ Jesus our Lord."

Christ is no 'fair weather' friend.
Inspired by the story of Peter, who took up Jesus' invitation to walk on stormy waters. (Find it in **Matthew's Gospel, Chapter 14: verses 22-32**.)

Sometimes we just need to be brave enough to step out of the boat. We are invited to walk on stormy waters with Jesus, not drown in them.

A little deadly weapon

It's not a WMD for sure,
 and it never makes the news.
But it still can be quite deadly,
and real forthright with its views.

It can fire bullets double quick,
which then truly make their mark.
They can leave behind great jagged wounds
that fester in the dark.

It can't be confiscated,
and a license not required.
We often don't pay any heed
to the weapon we've just fired.

We've all recited "sticks and stones"
in that old children's rhyme. *
The second line is not quite true,
we don't realise at the time.

We possess a powerful weapon,
which we often can keep hidden.
We can choose to keep it well controlled,
and make it do our bidding.

The tongue is such a little thing,
which can wound, or it can heal;
For it can with just a word or two
affect how others feel.

Therefore, we must be careful
with the words we choose to say.
The tongue can be a deadly weapon,
and we use it every day.

*" Sticks and stones may break my bones,
But names can never hurt me."

Weapons of war are lethal and deadly. Most of us have never fought in a war of combat, yet I, along with everyone I know, possess a double-sided weapon. It can wound or it can build up. It can fire deadly darts or it can pour out the healing balm of Gilead. We carry it around with us 24 hours a day; the tongue. In the New Testament James put it this way:

"When we put bits into the mouths of horses to make them obey us, we can turn the whole animal. Or take ships as an example. Although they are so large and are driven by strong winds, they are steered by a very small rudder wherever the pilot wants to go. Likewise, the tongue is a small part of the body, but it makes great boasts. Consider what a great forest is set on fire by a small spark. The tongue also is a fire, a world of evil among the parts of the body. It corrupts the whole body, sets the whole course of one's life on fire, and is itself set on fire by hell.

All kinds of animals, birds, reptiles and sea creatures are being tamed and have been tamed by mankind, but no human being can tame the tongue. It is a restless evil, full of deadly poison.

With the tongue we praise our Lord and Father, and with it we curse human beings, who have been made in God's likeness. Out of the same mouth come praise and cursing. My brothers and sisters, this should not be." **James 3:3-10.**

What kind of light are you?

On a lonely, dark road
a soul wanders lost, afraid
and not knowing what to do next –
Will he be there forever?
Is there no hope?
Then, through the dark night
a flashlight comes.
Someone to show him the way,
for He is not lost anymore.
What kind of light are you?

A power cut -
a solitary candle glows,
shedding its light where
more modern versions have failed;
powerless.
Only one, yet by its light
the darkness is dispelled.
Grateful for its simple pleasure,
we can forget to be sophisticated
for a while.
What kind of light are you?

A child wakes from a nightmare,
afraid of the images
that have torn her from sleep.
She reached out and there is light,
comfortingly near
from a bedside lamp.
Where there is light
there is no need to fear.
What kind of light are you?

A dark sky, noise, a crowd;
lots of fun and laughter.
A firework shoots up,
far away into the night,
lighting the sky
with its brief blaze of glory,
causing gasps of delight.
But soon, too quickly, it is gone.

And those who are gathered
have only a memory.
For it has left the source
of its light and power behind.
What kind of light are you?

"I lay under the stars watching the stars from the sky drift heavenward, and surrendered my life to Christ. I did not want to be as one of those sparks which burned brightly and then died and fell back to earth as dead ash. I wanted to be like the stars that burned forever."
(Jamie Buckingham - from his book, 'Risky Living: Keys to Inner healing.')
Copyright© 2013 Risky Living Ministries Inc. (Revised 2015)
Original publication 1976.

Matthew 5; 16: In the same way, let your light shine before others, that they may see your good deeds and glorify your Father in heaven.

Who are you, Lord?

You told us that You are the Way,
We call you friend and brother.
You are the lover of my soul,
You know me like no other.

Yet sometimes, still I turn away,
from who you really are,
for fear the price I still must pay,
don't make me go that far.

But You want me to know You more,
and wait to show the way,
to a place that's made for me alone,
where with You I can stay.

So, help me, Lord, spend time with you,
in the place where I belong.
To realise my whole life through
That when I'm weak, I'm strong.

I don't have to be perfect
to walk in faith not fear,
for You will keep Your promise
That always You'll be near.

I really want to know You, Lord,
to truly be Your friend,
and not to be found wanting,
when the world comes to its end.

Help me then deny my flesh,
the things I'd rather do.
Let me see their worthlessness
In the light that comes from You.

For Jesus, You are holy,
and that's how I must be.
Help me live and be like You,
until Your face I see.

Acts, chapter 9: 5:6. "'Who are You, Lord?' asked Saul. 'I am Jesus whom you are persecuting,' He replied".

We must never forget with whom we have to do.